Be

Let us check your readiness for General Data Protection Regulation (GDPR)

By Punit Bhatia

Disclaimer

The thoughts and ideas listed in this book are aimed to help the reader with a perspective on GDPR implementation and assist through defining steps to build or challenge his/her compliance roadmap. The thoughts or ideas are not legal opinions and shall have no legal liability whatsoever.

Further, the opinions, thoughts, and ideas mentioned in this book are the personal opinions of the author as an individual and do not have any correlation with any company or organization for which the author has worked or is working.

Disclosure

Copyright © 2017. All rights reserved. No part of this publication may be used, copied, reproduced, modified, distributed, displayed, stored in a retrieval system, or transmitted in any form by any means (electronic, mechanical, photocopying, recording or otherwise), without the prior written authorization of author.

"Because there is a law such as gravity, the universe can and will create itself from nothing."

-Stephen Hawking

TABLE OF CONTENTS

About this Book 7
Why this book? 9
Who Is the Ideal Reader of This Book? 14
How to make best use of this book? 15
Chapter One: GDPR Basics and Key Terms 1
Chapter Two: GDPR Principles and Key Building Blocks 13
Chapter Three: Track 1: Put the Basics in Place 32
Chapter Four: Track 2: Privacy-by-Design 45
Chapter Five: Track 3: Make an Inventory of Personal Data 57
Chapter Six : Track 4: Data Expiration 65
Chapter Seven: Track 5: Consent 72
Chapter Eight: Track 6: Data Subject Rights 78
Chapter Nine: Track 7: Data Transfers 90
Chapter Ten : Track 8: Demonstrate Transparency 98
Chapter Eleven : Track 9: Create Awareness and Training 106

Chapter Twelve : Track 10: Manage Complaints and Breach 115

Chapter Thirteen : Track 11: Sustainability 123

Chapter Fourteen: Moving Forward with Your GDPR Compliance Plan................... 132

Chapter Fifteen: Critical Success Factors in Implementing GDPR Successfully............ 143

Appendices 154

   1.   Checklist for Senior Managers/Executives............................ 154

   2.   Checklist for Assurance of a Comprehensive GDPR Implementation Plan....………………………………156

   3.   Data Inventory Checklist................ 163

   4.   Privacy Statement Checklist.......... 164

About the Author....................................... 166

Acknowledgements 168

About this Book

Compliance to the General Data Protection Regulation (GDPR) is mandatory for any business involved in dealing with the personal data of EU residents. Assuring that your compliance plan is correct is not something that should be left to chance. This book is designed to provide you with a step-by-step approach on how to structure a data protection plan to assure compliance with GDPR. For those who already have a plan, this book will help review it and assure that the focus is assigned onto the right priorities. This book will provide answers to the following questions:

- How to set your privacy and protection program?
- How to structure your core team and governance?

- What are the key roadmap tracks to ensure GDPR compliance?
- What are the critical factors to assure GDPR compliance?
- How to remain compliant in the longer term?

Taking the right steps in your journey to GDPR compliance is important. If you need a pragmatic approach in plain English with actionable suggestions, this book is for you.

Why this book?

Increasingly, senior executives and line managers are more and more concerned about the impact of the new General Data Protection Regulation (GDPR) that takes effect May 25, 2018. Most of them understand that this new law will have a huge impact on their business, but the extent and areas of impact are not always clear. This is especially important for those who are sponsors for the change initiative or responsible to drive compliance with this law. As they review their plans, they remain uncertain whether the current plans for compliance will be sufficient or are they missing something? They fail to achieve a solid understanding of the law and do not feel sufficiently knowledgeable to challenge their colleagues who are working on the compliance approach. Quite often, their GDPR knowledge is built upon the information shared by the very colleagues who are designing and presenting the GDPR compliance plans. In the best case, the best in class and most confident ones have attended a few events on GDPR. The story does not differ for those working on GDPR compliance plans because, up until now, there has been very limited information available in the market.

Consulting firms have recently started to bring forth their perspectives on GDPR; however, the truth is that most are talking to customers in order to learn (and develop) from them with the intention to improve what they are supposed to provide.

The truth is, when you are challenged to implement compliance to law, you need simple and clear explanations of the key requirements for compliance and step-by-step guidance on actions to take. This book has been designed and written with these considerations in mind, and provides a simple solution for a complex problem. And, this simple solution is provided in plain English with actionable suggestions. Hence, this book is your solution.

Through experience and observations, I have identified a clear knowledge gap between GDPR requirements and how to assure compliance through successful implementation. I have noticed that key stakeholders are aware of this gap and have demonstrated their willingness to learn the concepts, but lack of adequate resources and time to achieve results.

As an attendee or speaker at GDPR compliance events, I have always found the above as a recurring, common pattern. People are getting highly engaged with the GDPR articles and terminology, but consistently seem to miss out on the bigger picture and broader perspectives that are required in building or reviewing a compliance roadmap.

At the same time, I have observed that people have been attentive to my thoughts and positively vocal in expressing benefit of what I had to offer when speaking to them. This encouragement of colleagues and those whom I have met has encouraged me to share my knowledge as a bird´s eye view on what GDPR is, how it should be viewed, and what the key aspects for ensuring compliance are. Hence, through this book, my objective is to simplify the concepts and help you build an overall understanding GDPR which includes the building blocks, critical success factors, and the key tracks for a GDPR implementation plan. This is especially important now, as we are less than one year from required compliance. And, having this knowledge and broad perspective can be immensely helpful in reviewing and enriching your plans. For those who don't already have a plan, this will help you build an implementation plan much faster rate than you thought possible.

Last, but not the least, the content in this book has intentionally been kept to a minimum. It is my belief that once you understand the minimum, you can get maximum results by building on it yourself or through other sources.

This said, I welcome you to enjoy reading the easy way to implement and comply with GDPR.

Who Is the Ideal Reader of This Book?

The ideal reader of this book is any person who aspires to understand the General Data Protection Regulation from a layman's perspective and to be involved in compliance with GDPR for his/her organization. The book is particularly suited for Data Protection Officers, project managers, program managers, senior managers, and business stakeholders willing to achieve a successful implementation of GDPR.

How to make best use of this book?

Before we begin, I would like to suggest three points that will greatly increase the value you receive from this material.

First and foremost, I would recommend that you do not "see" this material as a book in the sense that it is something to be read once and put on a shelf afterwards. To begin, read it completely once, then refer back to it to define, review, or implement various parts of your implementation plan.

Second, the building blocks of GDPR, referred to as tracks, are not to be viewed as sequential activities, but as a set of broad actions or focus areas that can mostly run in parallel. Any track(s) that can run independently or which depend upon others are indicated explicitly. As a rule and unless stated otherwise, consider these tracks as bundled actions to be initiated, followed, and executed in parallel.

Third, I would like to be explicit: this is not legal advice, but my personal perspective on GDPR for any manager or executive. This does not have any correlation with organization for which I work or have worked, but is the sum total of what I observed and learned. Hence, expect this to provide you with the knowledge that you need to build your plans, review your plans, challenge your colleagues, and complement the knowledge you already have.

To make it easier for the reader, each chapter has a "Pro Tips" section at the end. These guidelines will make your implementation quicker and more effective.

And, if you take care of above, I am extremely confident that you will gain a better understanding of GDPR, what should be done, and how you can steer your organization by providing pragmatic solutions to achieve compliance with GDPR.

Chapter One: GDPR Basics and Key Terms

Objective: In this chapter, you will learn about the history, the basics, and the key terms associated with General Data Protection Regulation.

Let us start by quickly aligning ourselves on a common understanding of what the General Data Protection Regulation (GDPR) is and the key terms associated with this law. This will allow us to build an implementation approach in coming chapters.

To understand the General Data Protection Regulation, it is important to note that GDPR is not a completely new law, but a harmonized, modernized, and strengthened revision of the Data Protection Directive of 1995 (95/46/EC). Here, I use three important words. Let us emphasize on each of these.

1. ***Harmonization*** created a single set of rules across all member states in the EU. Thereby making it easier for companies to comply.
2. ***Modernization*** made the directive relevant to today's reality. In 1995, there was no iPhone®, no LinkedIn®, no Facebook®, no Twitter® and the internet was in its infancy. Personal data, its privacy, and the risks associated with it were different. The two situations, the one of 1995 and now, are so different that the rules of 1995 can no longer be applied.
3. ***Strengthening*** because it provided what individuals need to be empowered with rights, and organizations need to be held accountable.

Therefore, GDPR is a welcome change that strengthens rights of individuals, puts accountability upon organizations processing personal data, and provides powers to Data Protection Authorities for enforcement.

For those of you wondering what do the words *directive* and *regulation* mean, in simple terms, a *regulation* is a law and does not necessarily need to elaborated upon by individual member states; however, a *directive* is set of rules that must be elaborated upon and ratified as law by each member state. As stated, we have no need to get into legal aspects, but understanding key terms is essential.

GDPR is a regulation. As such, it does not require ratification from member states (unless a member state chooses to be more explicit or stringent). It becomes a legally binding law effective May 25, 2018.

This means, all businesses must enact fundamental changes to their data protection practices to ensure that their processes, policies, systems, and contracts conform to the new regulation. Let me assure you that if you have been compliant to directive of 1995, then the work is all about building upon what is already in place. Of course, there is a huge issue if you have not been compliant thus far. (sadly, many people I meet at events state that they are not completely compliant with 1995 directive.) Anyhow, let us stay focused on understanding GDPR before we start on implementation.

GDPR is a set of rules governing how the personal data of individuals is processed and is applicable to customers, employees, and supplier personnel who are residing in the European Union. In GDPR language, these individuals are referred as *data subjects*.

To form a deeper understanding of GDPR, we must first align on a few terms that will assist us in building a good foundation.

Term	Description
Personal Data	Any information relating to an identified or identifiable natural person
Data Subject	An identified or identifiable natural person
Processing	Any manual or automatic operation performed on personal data
Controller	An individual or entity which determines the purposes for and means of processing personal data
Processor	An individual or entity that processes personal data on behalf of the controller
Supervisory Authority	A public authority in a member state responsible for monitoring compliance with GDPR

Table: Key GDPR Terms

As these are important terms, let us understand better.

Personal Data

To simplify the definition of personal data, GDPR uses the term *"personal data"* to refer to any information that can be used to directly or indirectly identify the *"data subject"*. This includes but is not limited to identification numbers, IP addresses, CCTV footage, etc. Further, personal data like race, religion, health, biometric information, political association, criminal history, etc. are further classified as *"sensitive data"*.

Processing

"Processing" pertains to any operation performed on personal data. This constitutes any action like collecting, storing, using, sending, or deleting personal data. To be specific, collecting includes recording and

using includes retrieval, usage, modification, and combining or even linking data. So, if a call center has read-only access to your customers´ data in Asia, then it is still considered *"processing"* of personal data.

Controller and Processor

As organizations process the personal data of data subjects, they are classified as *"controller"* or *"processor"*. Controller refers to the organization or entity that determines the purposes and means of processing personal data (e.g., when processing employees' data, employers are considered controllers). Parties can be joint data controllers in certain circumstances. The processor is an organization or entity which processes personal data on behalf of the controller (e.g., IT providers hosting personal data for their clients are considered processors).

Supervisory Authority

"Supervisory Authority" is a public authority in a member state responsible for monitoring compliance with GDPR. This is typically a privacy commission in a member state. It may have different name in each country. For example, in the UK it is named the Information Commissioners Office, and in Belgium it is known as the Privacy Commission. Sometimes, this is also referred as the "Data Protection Authority". Thanks to GDPR, there will also be a European Data Protection Board which unites all the presidents of such local data protection authorities.

Who does GDRP apply to?

GDPR applies to all organizations across the world that process personal data of EU residents. Therefore, GDPR applies to all organization across industry sectors and around the globe if they process the personal data of data subjects who are EU citizens or residents.

What are the consequences of non-compliance?

Non-compliance to this law invites fines of up to € 20 million or 4 percent of global turnover, whichever is higher. Of course, these are maximum fines and a sanction would be applied gradually to an organization in violation of the law. For your needs, be aware that fines are significant and applied gradually. Legal counsel can help you with different details of the fines. My objective is to help you make a plan that reduces the probability of any fine(s) and demonstrate compliance upon official request. So, let us move away from fines and spend our energy on doing the right things.

What are the key dates in context of GDPR?

For those who love dates, the EU initiated a reform process in 2012, reached agreement on the new GDPR on December 15, 2015, and published it on May 4, 2016. Organizations were given two years to achieve compliance and must be ready by May 25, 2018. In short, the time to act is now.

Pro Tips:

- GDPR is an EU regulation.
- GDPR is not new, but an extension of the EU Privacy Directive of 1995.
- GDPR is a set of rules about how the personal data of individuals is processed.
- GDPR applies to all companies across the world that process personal data of EU citizens and residents.

- Individuals can be customers, employees, or supplier personnel.
- The controller is an entity that determines the purpose of processing.
- The processor is the entity that processes personal data on behalf of the controller.

Chapter Two: GDPR Principles and Key Building Blocks

Objective: In this chapter, you will learn about the principles and key requirements of GDPR.

Now that you understand key terms and some basics about General Data Protection Regulation, it is time to build on our conversation and talk about core principles of GDPR and the key requirements that constitute GDPR.

Principles

The following principles are core to GDPR and must be understood before implementation:

- **Lawfulness, fairness, and transparency:** Personal data must be processed lawfully, fairly, and in a transparent manner in relation to the data subject.

- **Purpose limitation**: Personal data must be collected for a specific, explicit, and legitimate purpose. Processing must be limited to this legitimate purpose only.
- **Data minimization:** Personal data must be adequate, relevant, and limited to what is necessary in relation to the purpose for which it is processed.
- **Accuracy:** Personal data must be accurate and kept up to date.
- **Storage limitation**: Personal data should only be retained only to the extent necessary. That is, personal data should be deleted once the purpose for which it was collected is fulfilled. Of course, certain applicable laws may require data to be retained longer. For example, most countries define a retention period for medical records in hospitals. So, in such

cases, those relevant laws need to be referred.

- **Integrity and confidentiality**: Personal data must be processed in a way that ensures appropriate security, including protection against unauthorized or unlawful processing. And, data should remain accurate and consistent while protection against unintended alterations.

Now, let us expand our understanding of GDPR further and dive more deeply into GDPR requirements. For this, I aggregate the GDPR requirements in 12 building blocks that can help you understand GDPR requirements in a structured manner.

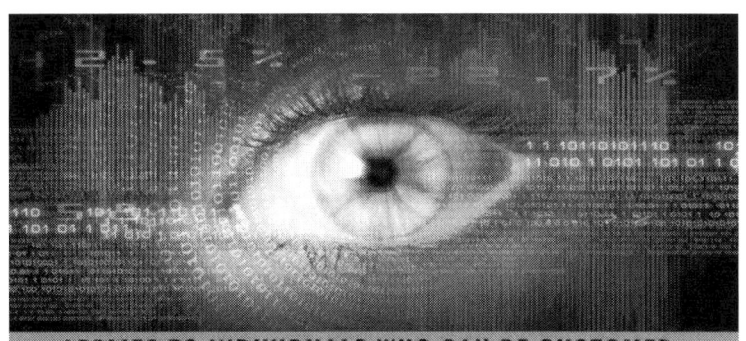

APPLIES TO INDIVIDUALS WHO CAN BE CUSTOMER, EMPLOYEE, OR PERSONNEL OF THIRD PARTIES.

1. Legitimate basis for data
2. Info you hold (retention)
3. Individuals' rights
4. Explicit and clear consent
5. Children's data
6. Privacy notices/statements
7. Data breaches
8. Privacy by design
9. Privacy impact assessment
10. Data protection officers
11. Third party management
12. Awareness

GDPR NON-COMPLIANCE CAN BE FINED UP TO 4% OF GLOBAL TURNOVER

Image: Key GDPR requirements

1. **Legitimate basis for data:** An organization must know and be able to prove that, for any processing it performs upon personal data, there is a legitimate purpose for doing so. For example, my internet provider has a reason to monitor my internet usage, because I signed an agreement to provide me internet and that entitles the internet provider to monitor usage, send invoices, process invoices, etc. Similarly, an employer has the right to process employees' payroll, because each employee signed an employment contract, and processing of that payroll is a legitimate purpose as per employment contract.

2. **Information you hold**: An organization should keep data only insofar as necessary. This means that if I paid back my mortgage

fully, but now only keep a bank account, then the bank has no reason to keep my mortgage history, details of my assets, salary, etc. Of course, the bank must respect other laws that pertaining to retention of mortgage data; however, the data should not be processed anymore.

3. **Individuals rights**: To be assured that personal data is protected, data subjects have the right to ask what information one has about them and what one does with it, to ask for correction, to object to processing, to lodge complaint, to withdraw consent, or even to request deletion of their personal data (although the last is not an absolute right). This means I can ask my internet provider to tell me what data they have about me and

request them to stop processing my data or to even delete it.

4. **Consent**: When processing personal data, there should be explicit and clear consent from the individual. This means, if you wish to perform an activity like analytics for the purpose of making personalized offers, then the concerned individual should ideally be asked to provide his or her consent. As part of consent request, you must state what you will do with the information. For example, this means if the internet provider intends to monitor the type of movies and websites I watch, then they should ask for my consent.

5. **Children´s data:** For processing of children's data, GDPR requires the explicit

consent of the child's parents (or guardian) for minors less than 16 years of age. In this case, member states can set a lower or higher age of consent, with a minimum at 13 years. This means, data processors should not send letters to my children just because they may know that I have children who may want to buy mobile telephones.

6. **Privacy notices**: Organizations must transparently state their approach to personal data protection in a privacy notice that is easily accessible to data subjects. This privacy notice should have clear and easily understood language. For example, on their website my telecom provider should provide me information on what data they have, what they do with it, and with whom they share it.

7. **Data breaches**: Organizations must maintain a data breach register and, based on risk the regulator and data subject should be informed within 72 hours of identifying the breach. For instance, if my telecom provider's systems are hacked, they should inform the supervisory authority and me if there is a risk to my data.

8. **Privacy by design:** Mechanisms to protect personal data should be incorporated in design of new systems and processes, so that privacy and protection aspects are ensured by default. This means an organization should execute principles and guidelines to ensure that business and IT systems (and processes) are built to protect data subjects' privacy from the very beginning of the design phase.

9. **Privacy impact assessment**: When initiating new initiatives like a project, campaign, or product that would process personal data, the organization must conduct a privacy impact assessment to review the impact and possible risks.

10. **Data Protection Officers**: The organization should, in certain circumstances, assign a Data Protection Officer whose name and contact are published on the organization's website and identified by the regulator so that he/she can be contacted by data subjects or regulators if or when required.

11. **Third parties**: The controller of personal data has the responsibility to ensure that personal data is protected and GDPR

requirements are respected, even if processing is performed by a third party. GDPR goes a step further in this aspect in that processors also have same obligations and liability as controllers in case of a data breaches.

12 <u>Awareness</u>: To create awareness among your staff about key principles on data protection, conduct regular training to ensure that the personal data of data subjects is protected and breaches are identified as soon as possible.

All of above can be summarized as follows: GDPR is a set of rules governing the treatment of the personal data of data subjects, while requiring organizations processing the data to be fully transparent in their use of that data. To ensure compliance, GDPR empowers the individuals (data subjects) with certain rights and holds organizations accountable for their actions. The regulator is also empowered to monitor compliance, resolve complaints, and issue sanctions or fines in case of non-compliance.

GDPR through example: Loyalty card

Let us understand these requirements using the following example to raise some interesting questions on compliance with GDPR from the customer's perspective. I choose the first example in retail industry, because it concerns all of us. We all go shopping, which puts our GDPR understanding and relevance under the spotlight. Imagine, you ask for a vendor's loyalty card, which requires that you fill a form. Typically, a customer loyalty form asks for your:

- Name
- Date of birth

- Address
- Mobile number
- Email
- Signature.

Is all this data truly required? To annoyance of some, I like to state that date of birth is not a required field. Of course, it helps to identify me, which can be argued as necessary. But, the reality is that the provider wants to know my age to build a profile on me but the exact date is not necessary. Instead, they can ask my age bracket which provides the same reliable data without being overly intrusive. Anyhow, let us assume I provide this information.

A few weeks later, I start receive brochures of monthly offers from this shop from I got a loyalty card from. Processing data for the loyalty card was a legal purpose, and sending marketing offers can be a legitimate interest. I take no action to unsubscribe because I like the discounts.

This gets more interesting. In six months, I discover that the offers sent to me and my neighbor are different. This means my shopping behavior is being tracked through use of the loyalty card. The question is, did I give consent to the processing of my shopping behavior linked through the loyalty card? Should I not have been asked before this action was executed? It is debatable if this personalization is a legitimate purpose or not. Again, let us assume that I choose not to act, because I like the personalization and can receive offers relevant to me.

Let's say another six months later, this company´s systems were hacked. News broadcasts state that all customers with loyalty cards have had their credit card numbers also hacked. This means my credit card may have been hacked and I need to know whether I should block my card. I go to the store's website to find information, but find nothing. I call the shop, but they state that such information details are not shared at the store level, and they are sorry, but they cannot help me. The hackers now have my credit card details and all personal information linked to the card, greatly facilitating any attempt to fraudulent use of the card.

Without piling on misery, let us see how this scenario would change if GDPR was correctly implemented. A compliant organization would have had the following changes:

- The data requested should have been limited to what was needed to provide the service. The actual date of birth was irrelevant to offer the Loyalty Card service and increased the harm caused by breach of security.
- The company should have made it clear on what grounds they would sending me marketing material.
- The company should have asked my consent to analyze my shopping behavior, so that offers could be personalized.
- The company should have sent me an email message assuring that my data had not been breached. Or, in a worst case, I received an email message stating my personal data had been breached, that the data was encrypted, and that the risk of fraud was low; but,

still they advised me to block my credit card to mitigate any risk.
- The company should have published the generic information on its website, and the store manager should have referred me to a helpline where I can raise questions.

Some of you may wonder whether all of this is common sense. Yes, it is. It is so common and ethical, that everybody knows. Perhaps, we expect organizations to do all of this. So, why make the fuss if GDPR comes into effect and demands organizations be ethical, transparent, and accountable—as they should be. And what happens if they are not, it is required to enforce the same through strong penalties and extended rights towards data subjects.

Next, as we align on implementation, it is important to realize that compliance with

GDPR involves multiple aspects and can become complicated if not structured appropriately. Hence, I recommend considering a structured approach similar to what will be described in coming chapters. You are free to call these *projects within your program* or *work streams in a project* or whatever makes you comfortable. For ease of discussion, let us call these *tracks*.

Pro Tips:

- GDPR has many articles that can be overwhelming to understand. These articles are very useful, but I recommend using the 12 building blocks described above (or a similar approach) for broad understanding so that you can be in control of your implementation.
- Similar to the loyalty card example, create scenarios within each of your

departments on how GDPR can impact you and to demonstrate how you may need to do things differently. This will make planning your implementation easier.

Chapter Three: Track 1: Put the Basics in Place

Objective: In this chapter, you will learn about the basics on how to set up your data privacy and protection program, engaging key stakeholders required for privacy implementation and the governance setup required to oversee the implementation.

The first step of any GDPR implementation puts in place a set of basics that builds a structure to your implementation. This direct focus toward a broad set of actions to executed for the successful implementation of GDPR. If not done well, GDPR implementation can get complicated, and stakeholders and sponsors will find it difficult to get a sense of what is going on. Take time to do this right.

Normally, based on your organization, this can take anywhere between one and four weeks. For the purpose of this book, I aggregate related set of actions into tracks. Putting the basics in place is the first track. The first track starts and continues until you complete the GDPR compliance process. In certain cases, it may continue afterward as well.

Now, let us get into the core of actions required in this track:

1. **Assign a Data Protection Officer (DPO)** with a clear mandate for your organization. This is a key requirement of GDPR, as this person would oversee the data protection strategy and its implementation. This person would also be your organization´s representative to regulators and data subjects for data protection and privacy issues. Your DPO

may not be a person with legal background. Further, for large organizations wherein layers of hierarchy segregate responsibilities, consider splitting this role between two or more people. You can have a DPO role focused on legal compliance and reporting, while another role for the first line of defense focuses on day-to-day guidance for business and technology stakeholders. Ideally, assigning a DPO is the first step to initiating a GDPR implementation plan. Some small organizations may decide not to assign a DPO. In that case, move to next step.

2. **Assign a program or project manager** to coordinate and manage the implementation plan and budget, to manage stakeholders, and to provide regular updates on progress. In my

experience, a hands-on program manager is best suited to steer this process.

3. **Identify the right stakeholders** who will contribute to and steer the GDPR implementation. This may include representation from business, marketing, data, risk, compliance, legal, architecture, IT, security, and project/program management teams. In a large enterprise, especially in heavily regulated industries, focus on having two sets of representatives per function. This allows for splitting the contribution and steering responsibility. It is vital to be explicit: the contribution responsibility includes regular participation and spending dedicated time to prepare, review, and validate the content aspects. The steering responsibility involves executive sponsorship and direction at the program level. It's worth mentioning

that contribution responsibility involvement can command as much as 50% of their total time. I fully understand that resources are precious and always in short supply; but, unfortunately, there are no shortcuts. I can only recommend that you initially assign representatives for contribution without specific commitment on dedicated of time. With time, the relevant representatives themselves will understand the need and required commitment. For small organizations, contribution and steering responsibilities may generally be combined, as would be the case of the representation of different departments. These contributing stakeholders become the GDPR core team for your organization in the longer term, while the those with steering responsibility serve as the executive steering group for GDPR.

4. **Setup governance**: As soon as the right stakeholders are identified, define and install a formal governance structure that drives the GDPR implementation (both on the project program levels). In most cases, a weekly content meeting with the GDPR core team (those having a contribution responsibility) and monthly steering committee meetings suffice. Establish an update and escalation procedure with the top-level executives of your organization. If you are working in a large organization with multiple entities, then you may need to decide on program structure; i.e., whether your program will provide central guidance or local guidance. Central guidance means all aspects are coordinated centrally; local units only implement guidelines. Local guidance means only the instruction to implement is central;

however, the rest of the decisions and implementation are locally determined within each entity. Clarify this in the governance. In my view, programs of increasing scale and complexity are best driven by a hybrid model; i.e., sufficient guidance centrally coupled with detailed guidance on crucial topics.

5. **Set up the GDPR core team**: List the key aspects of GDPR that apply to your organization. This can be referred to as defining a data protection charter similar to any project or program charter that lays out the basic structure of what you will do, why you will do it, who is needed, and when.

6. **Define your data protection policy**: For a really large organization with operations in multiple countries, it makes sense to do this action in two parts: a central interpretation of GDPR and

statements on how different countries need to comply with GDPR. In that case, the company level charter is best referred as a data protection policy for the organization which must be implemented by each country through its individual program. This approach has two benefits: 1) you avoid interpretation of GDPR at each country level; 2) you set the tone by providing common guidance and a cohesive approach on how each country should act. In this case, each country must act to ensure compliance to the organization's internal data protection policy, while the central team takes responsibility for interpretation of GDPR. Either way, whether you define a policy at company, charter, country, or organization level, you must reuse the information listed in different tracks mentioned in this book. I believe all the tracks mentioned in this book are relevant for most organizations intending to comply with GDPR. There can, of course, be exceptions and variances in the way you want to do things. Having said so, there is no point reinventing the wheel; therefore, I strongly recommend using these tracks unless you already have an ongoing implementation plan. In that case, you should use this book to validate the completeness of your plan. Either way, it is critical to review each track based on the needs of your organization and decide whether to split, aggregate, and/or not implement some aspects in collaboration with your core team, as necessary.

7. **Build a data protection program charter**: Once you have identified the different tracks applicable to your organization (you may use any name you

wish, but I will use this term for the sake of consistency and easy reference), decide on three different dimensions; i.e., data subjects. By this, I mean, for each track, articulate what work is involved relating to customer, employee or supplier personnel data.

8. **Assign an executive sponsor**: An executive sponsor from the executive committee should be assigned to oversee GDPR implementation. Next, to bring further accountability to your charter, assign an executive sponsor per each track per type of data subject. For each track, articulate what work relating to customer, employee, or supplier personnel data is involved. This may be an unnecessary step for small and mid-sized organizations and ignored. However, this step is crucial for large

organizations and should be done diligently.

9. **Make a plan or roadmap:** As soon as your data protection charter is ready, make a roadmap or plan and start following it until all the actions are completed. As you do so, keep documented evidence of what you decide, why, and when. This evidence helps demonstrate, if required, that your organization has a structured approach towards data protection and privacy. Remember that plan will need to be reviewed and refined as you progress.

10. **Allocate budget:** once you have a plan, you can review and allocate a budget for the scheduled activities. The budget will need to be refined once you have completed a gap analysis and actions have been prioritized.

In summary, track one is all about putting in place the basics like assigning a DPO, onboarding the right stakeholders, defining a charter, and setting up the correct governance to steer your GDPR implementation. These are the basic principles of managing any program or project, but nuances of GDPR mandate almost all the departments of your organization be involved.

Also, this track is the most fundamental and important track. It will start first and, most likely, end the last.

Pro Tips:

- The Data Protection Officer role is full-time role in large organizations. Some organizations prefer to assign an external DPO to ensure neutrality and to pay only for the days you need the service.
- Putting the basics in place is the beginning, not the end.

- Document and retain records of all decisions made in this and subsequent tracks.
- Engaging relevant stakeholders from start will have significant benefit from long-term perspective.

Chapter Four: Track 2: Privacy-by-Design

Objective: In this chapter, you will learn how to initiate real actions, set the foundations for privacy by design, and set up a Data Privacy Impact Assessment. This will move you forward with your GDPR compliance.

Once the basics have been put into place, start with the requirement of privacy-by-design. The privacy-by-design requirement demands that each new initiative that makes use of personal data take the protection of such data into consideration. Also, an organization must be able to show that it has put adequate security in place and that compliance is monitored. In practice, this means that each initiative must take privacy into account during the entire life cycle of the system or process development. Privacy-by-design complements this by engaging the strictest privacy settings to be automatically applied once a data subject acquires a new product or service.

For me, this is done in three simple steps:

1. To cover the existing processes and systems in the organization, conduct a business and technical gap analysis immediately.
2. To ensure that each new initiative remains within the boundaries of privacy and protection principles, mandate that each initiative that includes processing of personal data go through a Data Privacy Impact Assessment (DPIA).
3. To standardize the required actions and mechanisms that protect personal data, define the privacy-by-design guidelines for systems.

Now, let us understand each of these three steps in detail.

Gap analysis at business and technical levels

One of the crucial aspects of setting your GDPR implementation in motion is to conduct a gap analysis, because it helps set a baseline on the current situation in the organization. Generally, an organization would perform a gap analysis at both the business and IT levels. The business gap analysis focuses on identifying gaps in policy and procedures that exist on the business side, while the technical gap analysis focuses on identifying gaps where technical systems and applications need to be adapted. Further, a business gap analysis is conducted per business unit/department, while the technical gap analysis is conducted per application (IT system). To optimize efforts, I would recommend first focusing on business units and technical systems that process personal data, then conducting analyses on the remaining ones later.

Some consultants even advise a process gap analysis that reviews each process and then identifies gaps. I believe that business and technical gap analyses, if done well, identify the process gaps.

Although gap analysis is important, but this exercise should not mean that no other action can be taken until you have identified all the gaps. You can take a layered approach to this (e.g., the first process level and then the application level or a hybrid sample model). If you do delay action until all gaps are identified, there is a significant risk that you may not have enough time to act post-gap analysis. A typical gap analysis on the business or technology side should take between three to six weeks. You are better off not to lose those weeks. Further, I strongly believe that both business and technical gap analyses can be conducted simultaneously. However, if for some reason you need to choose, then the business gap analysis should be conducted first. To conduct a gap analysis, you may create your own questionnaire; but, I would recommend buying this as a service, because almost all consulting firms have spent energy on building standard templates which can be used instead of reinventing the wheel. While I do recommend using external help for gap analysis, I like to emphasize that your GDPR implementation should ideally be steered internally to set the right conditions to drive and keep control.

Data Privacy Impact Assessment (DPIA)

To ensure that privacy and protection are embedded by default, use a Data Privacy Impact Assessment (DPIA) questionnaire. The objective of this questionnaire is to monitor and evaluate the impact of new initiatives on personal data processing of data subjects in line with GDPR requirements. I recommend that each new initiative—like a new project, program, product, or campaign that gets launched—should be required to go thru a DPIA. This way you ensure that new initiatives do not create new gaps and that the necessary steps are systematically taken to ensure compliance.

Again, you may create your own DPIA, but I would not recommend so because almost all consulting firms have spent significant effort in employing certain best practices in building standards that can be used off the shelf.

Ideally, a DPIA should have following elements:

- Confirm that processing is within legitimate purposes. If not, consent from the data subject is procured.

- Clarify if rights of data subjects are impacted. If so, determine what action is needed.
- Confirm that required security measures to protect personal data are in place. If not, determine what actions need to be taken.

I have observed some consultants or organization refer to both gap analysis and DPIA as DPIA; however, that may create confusion with stakeholders. To me, it is much simpler to say that we do a gap assessment at the organization and system levels and ask each new (relevant) initiative to go through DPIA. Regardless of your preference, be clear and communicate the choice you make.

Privacy-by-design guidelines

Based on your data protection charter (or policy), you should ask your architect to put together a set of standard guidelines. This helps standardize the required actions and mechanisms that help protect personal data in new and existing systems. This includes setting certain principles and lays out certain options on what and how. For example, a new application being designed should be asked to ensure protection of data by encryption of data in case data is shared on internet. Further, this can provide guidance on which encryption technology and techniques to use. Again, in certain large organizations, architects recommend creating two level of such guidance. One is exclusively focused on *what* (e.g., saying you should use encryption in this case) and another is exclusively focused on *how* (e.g., detailing what encryption technology be used). That may be more effective for some, but I emphasize having a single privacy-by-design guideline that is clear and actionable. Ideally, these guidelines should cover:

- What is the approach towards masking data? Which IT environments will mask the data?
- When should anonymization or pseudonymizing be used? How will this be performed?
- When and how should access rights to the personal data of data subjects be restricted?
- What are the protection measures (e.g., scrambling, minimization) that need to be put in place before data is analyzed for analytics purposes?
- How is confidentiality, integrity, and availability of personal data assured?
- How are privacy choices enabled by default? (For example, opt-in options are

not ticked-in by default, but customer has to choose.)

Once your privacy-by-design guidelines are available, you will have a fair view of the key IT actions required for securing personal data. Typically, these actions must:

- ensure the confidentiality of personal data by preventing unauthorized access to personal data;
- ensure the integrity of personal data by executing measures that prevent unauthorized or unintentional alteration or deletion of personal data;
- ensure that availability of data for authorized users is guaranteed in line with requirements; and,
- ensure sufficient traceability on processing of personal data.

In summary, gap analysis, Data Privacy Impact Assessments, and privacy-by-design guidelines are important instruments to demonstrate that your organization has fulfilled its accountability in establishing and maintaining data privacy.

Pro Tips:

- Privacy by design guidelines must be embedded. This is a behavioral change and takes time.
- The concept of privacy-by-design comes from Canada (Information and Privacy Commissioner of Ontario). Look into that for a deeper understanding of what is expected.
- Pseudonymizing is substitution of identifiable data with a other values while anonymization is the destruction of the identifiable data. This means Pseudonymization is reversible while

anonymization is irreversible. Consequently, pseudonymized data is still personal data because it can be identified if reversal key is obtained.

- Keep evidence of the gap analysis and privacy impact assessments that are conducted. This evidence will be extremely useful if you are asked by a regulator to demonstrate the accountability principle of GDPR.
- A gap analysis may be conducted regularly (every alternate year would be practical) to remain in control of risks and gaps.
- Consult ISO 27001, 27002, or 27018 for standards and refer to the principles of information security management. These security standards can assist in the protection of personal data.

Chapter Five: Track 3: Make an Inventory of Personal Data

Objective: In this chapter, you will understand how to make an inventory of personal data, the right level of capturing inventory, and how to make your inventory fulfill the key requirements of GDPR.

If you recall the building blocks of GDPR, then you know it is critical to be in control of what personal data your organization has, which processes it uses, and why and how long that data is kept. As most organizations have this information scattered in different documents and systems, it is imperative to conduct an inventory of personal data. This will not only help you take necessary action within the context of GDPR, but it can also be a strategic step, because it will eventually help your organization understand the wealth of personal data that exists and bring forth ideas to further leverage your big data analytics and your digitization approach. For now, we shall focus on what we need from the GDPR perspective, because leveraging data for analytics and digitization are vast topics that deserve separate books. If you have a data department in your organization, then it is possible that it may have some sort of data inventory upon which you can build. For simplicity, let us build one from scratch.

The purpose of a GDPR-based data inventory is to understand what data you have, where is it processed, and how it flows. A good data inventory should answer the following questions for each data category:

- What personal data you have in each business process?
- What type of data is this? Normally, classifying personal or sensitive is enough, but you may choose to define a

deeper classification if you believe that adds more value.

- Which data subject does this pertain to? Here, you classify whether data belongs to customers, employees, or supplier personnel.
- What is the purpose of this data? Consider making a standard list of processes that your organization carries out and map each data type to one of those.
- How long is this data stored? Specify whether the data is stored in paper or electronic format.
- How long should you legally keep this data? This is tricky and depends upon the advice of your legal counsel as you must choose which law applies.
- When does the data storage timeline start? This is also tricky, because you need to agree with business and legal

experts on when the storage period for this specific data begins.

- What is the role of your organization in context of this data? Recall controller and processor roles we spoke about earlier. Here, you need to classify if your organization is playing the role of processor or controller.
- Is this data shared outside the country in which it is captured? If so, you need to keep record of the country to which it is transferred, and may need to take other necessary actions.
- Who are the processors involved in this data?
- Which applications process this data?

If your data inventory structure includes all of the above elements, then you do not need to invest in keeping retention schedules, because you are already capturing retention, or storage, information. This will save you time later on. Some organizations tend to take inventory without any information on storage or retention. Doing that sets yourself up for another iteration of revisiting all stakeholders to capture how long data is (and should be) stored and when the retention period starts.

From my experience, the data inventory is best captured at the aggregated business term level, not IT field level. For example, capturing the address of a customer at the time of customer onboarding is more relevant than fine-grained information like street name, house number, postal code, etc. Furthermore, the aggregated information is business-relevant. Consultants and available tools generally recommend scanning IT systems to create a data inventory. I am not in favor of this for following reasons:

- Scanning systems create lot of data that business stakeholders may not understand and hence not provide additional the information that you need from a business perspective.
- Such data may not have any business value and would remain difficult to maintain.
- Any such scan will only provide part of the information you need to capture in data inventory.

In short, scanning data creates more questions than answers. Aside from that, you may end up having an inventory of limited value for business and which remains in IT for maintenance.

Pro Tips:

- Data inventory is best captured at the aggregated business term level, not the IT field level.
- Data inventory is best captured by business teams, while IT teams can assist, if required, to fill certain elements.
- The best way to capture data inventory is to go through customer journeys or business processes, one by one, and fill the data used in each. This means you may have certain data repeating for different processes; however, that makes it easier to manage retention and processing information.
- As a rule of thumb, the data storage period should be determined according to the law with maximum storage allowed.
- While capturing a data inventory is important, it is more important to keep it

up to date on a regular basis as GDPR will stay. One exercise won't suffice. For this, you are better off investing in a software package that can help maintain this information.

- If captured with business stakeholders, and at the right level, the data inventory can become an important asset to help your business make decisions in future.
- Data inventory can be one among the first set of activities and does not have to wait for input, unless your organization has the data inventory already.
- The data inventory approach stated in this chapter allows you to fulfill requirements to register processing activities, retention schedules, and a list of processors.

Chapter Six : Track 4: Data Expiration

Objective: In this chapter, you will learn how to plan for the expiration of data once inventory has been made. This is very important and not done in most cases, because once data is stored, it remains forever. Implementing this well can bring cost savings, too.

As you capture the data inventory, the storage information will likely reveal that data is being retained post the legally relevant storage period. This is the case for most organizations, as well as a challenge from the perspective of GDPR compliance. One must realize that beyond compliance, this creates significant costs in the storage, maintenance, and security of data that one does not need (and perhaps no one ever needs).

As per GDPR, personal data should no longer retained when the purpose of processing the data ceases to exist. For organizations with a long history and old systems, this is very challenging to implement because we are not in "paper days" when *delete* means the paper is torn off, shredded, or burned and the action cannot be reversed. Instead, we are in digital world wherein *delete* can be defined as:

- Inactivated: Data exists but is not in active processing.
- Soft Delete: Data is marked for deletion, but remains in the system.
- Archived: Data is moved to another system where it remains with access restricted to some key stakeholders.
- Permanent Delete: Data is destroyed and cannot be recovered.

To address this challenge, a data expiration approach needs to be prepared and agreed upon. Consider using guidance from supervisory authorities. Some supervisory authorities have published guidelines on their websites. A data expiration approach should constitute of:

- What action is to be executed once data is past the required storage or retention period?
- Who will approve such action and, on what basis? Normally, the retention period listed in your data inventory can be a firm basis if agreed upon by relevant stakeholders.
- A decision on whether the expiration action is reversible or irreversible? Given the latest technologies, it is always possible to reverse a certain action. Do you want such reversibility? Is so, under what conditions?

- Who shall be notified when such action is taken? This is another challenge, because you cannot say I acted on data once it was beyond its legitimate retention period. As you are accountable, you need to track all received this data during the active lifecycle and notify them that similar actions must be taken on their end. And, it is this challenge that makes the permanent deletion almost impossible to execute.
- How will these actions be documented? This is very important. Imagine you remove data, but cannot track the action. If you are in a highly regulated industry such as finance or pharmaceuticals, then a regulator may ask you to prove what was done, when, and why. Therefore, having an audit trail would be handy.

Once your data expiration approach is ready, it must be approved by the executive committee, because this can have serious consequences for your organization. These consequences can range from an impact on your analytics plans, reporting to the industry regulator, and or being in a position to respond to enquiries in the longer term. Once approved, the technical solutions that will enable this approach need to be determined and made available.

Next, in terms of action on expired data, it is impractical (at least in my personal view) to expect that you can take expiration action on all personal data by May 2018. So, as soon as you have a data inventory, review the retention gaps and prioritize where immediate action is required to ensure that protection principles are respected. I recommend a risk-based approach towards these actions, rather than planning and initiating wholesale actions all at once.

Pro Tips:

- Data expiration actions need to be taken in consideration of all laws that apply.
- Review data expiration decisions carefully. Certain approaches are irreversible and can create irreparable damage. Hence, it is important to make no choices you'll regret.
- Where possible, you may consider aligning your data expiration approach with a regulator. Having said so, I understand the challenges associated with that. Hence, it is important you weigh the consequences of doing so, or not.
- The data expiration approach can be worked upon from the beginning of GDPR implementation, and it is needed

by the time you have reviewed the data inventory and identified the gaps. This is one more action to start early.

Chapter Seven: Track 5: Consent

Objective: In this chapter, you will learn the particulars of consent, the requirements for consent, when consent is required, and, more importantly, when it is not required. As you read, always remember a customer can withdraw consent.

As per GDPR, when processing personal data for any purpose other than legitimate purpose that data subject signed for, explicit and clear consent be requested. Unlike the past practice, consent cannot now be asked through pre-ticked or silent opt-in. Let us first understand key aspects of consent in GDPR:

- Consent must be for a specific purpose.
- Consent must be freely given.
- Consent must be unambiguous.

- Consent is only valid if the data subject is at least 16 years old (can be different under local law).
- Consent cannot be linked to provisioning of a service or product.
- Consent has to be explicit and pre-ticked boxes may not be used.
- The data subject should be able to withdraw consent at any time.
- Consent must be verifiable. The burden of proving that consent was procured rests upon controller. This implies a need to have some sort of record of the fact that consent was provided.

It is important to realize that consent is one of the means to process personal data and not the only one. So, let us review some scenarios where a consent is not required:

- When there is a contractual agreement in place to process personal data. For example, if your customer signed an insurance contract, then you have a legitimate purpose: i.e., execution of the insurance contract.

- When the activity is critical to your business and an objection from the customer would limit your ability to provide the service. For example, you need to secure your insurance liability by reinsuring all your contracts with a reinsurer. In this case, sharing required personal data with a reinsurer is acceptable, as it is critical to execution of insurance contract.
- When action is taken to protect the customer data. For example, encrypting all personal data in your systems to ensure that data remains protected.
- When action is core to your own business interest. For example, you

- have to share certain credit or default information with a regulatory agency.
- When you are acting in best interests of individual. For example, an employee has heart attack and you call an ambulance, share personal details, and ensure that the employee's life is protected.

However, analyzing personal data to make direct marketing offers may not be agreed upon in the contractual agreement and cannot be critical to performing the services agreed to in contract. In this case, explicit consent would be required, unless your organization classifies marketing as a legitimate interest. It remains debatable whether supervisory authorities will accept this such reasoning; but, for now, this can be one such option. Irrespective of what approach you choose, it is important that a decision be made for your organization and that you following the documented approach. Be aware that exceptions to the consent tend to be interpreted very restrictively.

In terms of timing, work on your approach towards consent can start immediately. This is best done by your marketing team in collaboration with key stakeholders. It is likely to be identified as a gap by the business gap analysis, so it's best to start now instead of waiting for the gap analysis report. This will allow you to save time later.

Pro Tips

- Remember that consent can be withdrawn at any time. So, be very sure that your processing can be stopped based on withdrawal of consent.
- As consent is withdrawn, you may need to notify a third party processing the data if such processing is outsourced.

- Acceptance of cookies is also equivalent to consent. So, review your cookie approach and make changes where necessary.
- Even though it is not explicitly stated, you may consider not obtaining fresh consent if you have been compliant with 95 Privacy Directive.

Chapter Eight: Track 6: Data Subject Rights

Objective: In this chapter, you will learn how to set up your GDPR program, how to identify the key stakeholders required for GDPR implementation, and create a governance procedure to oversee implementation.

GDPR provides data subjects with rights on their personal data. These rights include:

Right to Information

This implies that, as a data subject, I want transparency on what personal data you have and how is my personal data processed. As long as you publish a privacy statement in the right way (described in the next chapter), you should be covered. At the same time, it is important that the data subject be duly informed about existence of a privacy statement.

Right to Access

This implies that, as a data subject, I want to have access to my personal data. Your organization is obliged to provide a copy of this information upon request and at no cost to the data subject. However, you may charge a reasonable fee—or even refuse to share information—if requests are repetitive and/or unnecessary. Should you refuse to provide the requested information, you must inform that data subject that he/she/it has the right to lodge a complaint with the supervisory authority. Typically, the starting point for this information would be personal data shared in a profile page that is usually accessible when a customer logs into your portal. For further requests by data subject, your organization can even ask for one or two months (based on complexity) before providing a response.

Right to Rectification

This implies that, as a data subject, I have the right to ask for modification of incorrect or incomplete information. In case of a complex request, an extension of the timeline is feasible, but such a request must be made to the data subject. Once again, you can choose to refuse to rectify; but, you will need to inform the data subject that he/she has the right to lodge a complaint with the supervisory authority. Normally, the starting point to implement this law would be to let data subjects modify their personal data shared in profile pages that are usually accessible when a customer logs into your portal. More detailed and complex requests can be managed manually.

Right to Object

This implies that, as a data subject, I can object to processing of my personal data for direct marketing, research, etc. This is a generally a case of withdrawal of consent, unless you have listed marketing as a legitimate interest. If so, the data subject would need to be removed from direct marketing. Typically, this should be implemented online and through his or her profile page.

Right to Object to Automated Decision making

This implies that, as a data subject, I can request for human intervention when subjected to automated decisions. This allows data subjects to avoid the risk of potentially damaging decisions when and where there is no human intervention. Typically, this can be enabled by identifying scenarios in which your organization relies completely upon automated decisions and allows data subjects to demand human intervention in unfavorable decisions.

Right to Restriction

This implies that, as a data subject, I may request a block on processing of my personal data. When this right is exercised, the personal data remains with your organization, but processing of it should be restricted. Typically, this would be a case in which the data subject believes that processing is unlawful, or there is an ongoing legal proceeding. In my view, a typical implementation would be to flag the personal data as restricted for processing, and to ensure no active processing takes place.

Right to data portability

This implies that, as a data subject, I can request to obtain my personal data back, so that I can reuse the same data for the purpose of buying services from other organizations. Basically, it's a mechanism similar to mobile number portability (being offered by telecom operators), but effective across industries. When this right is exercised, you should provide the personal data in electronic format that is machine readable. This information must be provided free of charge. Eventually, it will evolve to individuals asking to transfer data from one organization to another, but that will take time. For now, the simplest way of implementing this would be provide the data in CSV format. Of course, this will change as organizations agree on standard formats for data exchange and transfers, because this will open huge opportunities while also making things easier for data subjects.

Right to Erasure

This is also often referred to as "Right to be Forgotten." This implies that, as a data subject, I can request deletion or removal my personal data if there is no valid reason for processing my data. Typically, "no valid reason" is logically construed as processing of data past the point for which the purpose the data was originally collected has been fulfilled. For example, once a mortgage has been fully paid to the bank, there is no reason for the bank to know details of my financial assets. This is not an absolute right and can be refused if the data in question needs to be retained for a legal reason, a legitimate purpose, for public interest, etc. To implement this right effectively, your data expiration approach would be a pre-requisite and serve as guidance on implementation.

In addition, there are a few common things that apply to all of the above:

- Whenever one of the above laws is exercised and one or more third parties act as processor, your organization must make a request for similar action by third party. Such third-party request must be done within one month. In case of complex requests, an extension of up to two months may be permitted.
- Your organization has the right to refuse the data subject's request if you conclude that request is repetitive or unnecessary or inhibits your organization's legitimate interests. Should you refuse a request, the data subject must be informed that he/she

has the right to lodge a complaint with a supervisory authority.
- These rights are relative to situations and are not absolute in nature. It is important to be clear on the scenarios wherein rights can be granted. For example, I cannot go to my bank and ask it to forget me, or stop processing my data, because I have an account and processing of my personal data is a legitimate interest under the contract signed when opening the account.
- GDPR allows the charging of fees in case of excessive requests.

It can be challenging to implement these rights. I agree and share an example to prove this. Imagine you are shopping at a grocery store and believe that something suspicious may have happened. To validate your suspicion, you exercise your right to access and ask for a copy of video surveillance. Now, your demand is perfectly legitimate and the store must comply at no cost to you. But, as an organization, I cannot provide you a video copy, because I need to protect privacy of others in the store. So, one solution is to blur images of others in the store and provide a modified copy. This is a significant cost and investment for the organization.

The purpose of sharing this example is not to state complexity and instill fear, but to emphasize the need for pre-identifying such scenarios and the corresponding solutions. Once done, you need to onboard key business stakeholders to agree upon a risk-based approach as to what is reasonably permitted by your organization, what would be refused, and what would be charged. This is another action that can happen right from start and does not have to wait for any other action.

In terms of timing, work on your approach towards data subject rights can also start immediately. This is best done by a customer experience team in collaboration with key stakeholders. It is also likely to be revealed by the business gap analysis. I recommend starting now instead of waiting for the gap analysis report. This will allow you to save time later.

Pro Tips

- Be pragmatic, think what a rational and logical customer would need, and implement these structurally.
- Imagine what a disgruntled customer can ask, and prepare some standard responses and escalation procedures.
- Be clear on situations when you will refuse requests. Make a list of such scenarios and publish them on your

website. This demonstrates transparency.
- Make agreements with third parties acting as processors to ensure their action when a right is exercised.
- While rights are available to all data subjects, put first priority on customers. In my view, it is relatively less likely that supplier personnel or an employee will demand the right to erase or object processing. So, taking a risk based approach, you can manage the rights for supplier personnel and employees as next step.

Chapter Nine: Track 7: Data Transfers

Objective: To help you organize the part of personal data processing that is not performed within your organization. This includes data managed with third party providers and inter- or intra-company entities.

In a globalized environment where companies focus on delivering core activities internally, it is natural that a significant number of services and processes are outsourced to other organizations. Some of these organizations may be entities within the same global organization or external providers that provide benefits in cost, efficiency, and or skill advantage.

You may recall from chapter 1 (*Chapter One: GDPR Basics and Key Terms*)that, in terms of

GDPR, when two organizations are involved, one that determines the purpose of processing is defined as the *controller* and the one that processes personal data on behalf of controller is defined as the *processor*. The good thing about GDPR is that it imposes the same liability, in terms of fines, on both controllers and processors. However, the controller has the accountability to ensure that processor fulfills its part of GDPR liability. Therefore, it becomes extremely important that expectations are clearly articulated in a formal manner. For this, there are two broad scenarios:

1. **Intra-company**

    Intra-company refers to the transfer of personal data within legal entities that are part of same parent company engaged in the exchange personal data for processing. For this, one can leverage on contractual clauses or Binding Corporate Rules (BCRs). While contracts as instruments to clarify responsibilities are well known, BCRs are internal rules or "codes of conduct" that a global company uses to define data transfer within the same corporate entities; i.e., inter-company. Hence, for large and global organizations, the definition of an internal data protection policy (the one which "puts basics in place") can serve as BCR. BCRs confer advantages like saving the effort of signing contracts for each data transfer and having a harmonized approach across same corporate entity.

2. Third Parties

When processing of personal data externally through third parties, it is important for formalize responsibilities in contracts. This means existing contracts need to be modified. A simple approach can be to define standard clauses required for data protection in line with GDPR and amend the contracts with the supplier who processes personal data on your behalf.

Include the following in your contracts:

- Definition and classification of personal and sensitive data.
- A list of the type of personal data and the categories of data subjects.
- Agreement by both parties to comply with General Data Protection Regulation.
- Definition of the responsibilities of the third party as "controller" or "processor".

- A request that the third party adopt, implement, and maintain requisite technical and organizational measures to contain risks inherent to processing of personal data for protection and prevention of accidental or unlawful destruction, loss, alteration, access, or unauthorized disclosure.
- Agreement by the third party not to transfer personal data to another party or country without the written consent of your organization. In doing so, the third party contracted to your organization will have to take responsibility and be liable of any such decision.
- Requirement of the third party to notify you of any breach, minor or major, without delay. In case of breaches, the third party is liable to customer.

- Requirement that the third party notify you of any request for disclosure of personal data by regulator (the organization that is asking for processing).
- Reservation of the right to audit the third party's data protection practices and to ask for a certification of compliance as and when required.
- Requirement that the third party delete all data (unless applicable law requires storage of personal data), and its copies when the contract is terminated.

Further, it is worth noting that the transfer of personal data to countries outside the European Economic Area (EEA) remains forbidden even in GDPR. However, the GDPR improvement is that you no longer need to notify data protection authorities when transfers are based on standard contract clauses. Having said that, the commission has determined certain countries as having sufficient data protection policies and this list is available on website of European commission.

This is another of the tracks that can be started immediately. This work is best completed by your procurement team. Of course, business teams need to be informed and need to own this while procurement provides support. The business gap analysis will likely identify this gap. I recommend starting now, instead of waiting for gap analysis report. This will allow you to save time later.

Pro Tips

- Bundle your standard contract clauses in line with GDPR into a data protection schedule or chapter that can then be included as an amendment to existing contracts. Such schedule or chapter can

then also be included into future contracts.
- Present your contract clauses to third parties as soon as possible. Otherwise, you will soon receive different versions as standards and end up with variety of clauses and no negotiation power.
- Instead of investing yourself in auditing or checking your suppliers' compliance to data protection principles, rely on security certifications from credible companies that perform such assessments and provide such assurance. Most large suppliers will generally obtain certification from multiple parties, as it helps them acquire more business.

Chapter Ten : Track 8: Demonstrate Transparency

Objective: To help you start demonstration of transparency towards individuals through use of privacy notices and statements.

First and foremost, some people confuse privacy statement, privacy notice, or privacy policy as the same. A *privacy policy* is your organization's internal guideline stating how your organization manages privacy. A *privacy statement* or *notice* is a customer (or employee or supplier personnel) document that assures the concerned party about how your organization manages their data.

Being transparent and allowing data subjects to have access to information is core of GDPR. The most common method to achieve that is to publish a privacy statement. A privacy statement should fundamentally answer a data subject's basics concerns:

- What personal data do you have about me? Why do you have this data?
- What do you do with this personal data? Basically, for what purposes do you use my personal data? Do you really need all the data you collected?
- Is this personal data shared outside of your company? If yes, with whom?
- What do you do with my data when it is no longer relevant?
- How do you respect privacy and protection of my data?
- What about my rights?
- Whom do I contact if I want to know more or lodge a complaint?

In short, a data subject wants assurance that his/her data is in safe hands and will be used for purposes intended, that his/her rights are respected, and that enough is being done to keep data protected in a structured manner.

A privacy statement for customers and supplier personnel is best published on your website with easy access. For an employee, it is best to publish your privacy statement on an intranet. Some organizations may choose to publish a privacy statement for supplier personnel via intranet, and that is also okay. Further, publication of a privacy statement should be combined with communication toward data subjects. This can include emails, information on the home page of your website, etc. The objective is to be transparent and to let customers know that something has changed or has been adapted. Last but not least, expect questions on your privacy statements as part of data subject rights and be prepared to answer them.

Privacy Notices

While privacy statements provide the standard information, organizations may have ad-hoc actions on the personal data of data subjects. These can include: reviews in case of data breach, responding to regulatory queries, etc. To ensure complete transparency in such circumstances, an organization should create a dedicated communication on website and state this as a privacy notice. Most experts use the terms *privacy statement* and *privacy notice* interchangeably; but, for me, the privacy statement is all about standard information concerning the *what*, *how*, and *who* of personal data processing, while the privacy notice is more about communicating immediate or one-off changes. For example, due to a breach or regulator's demand, you may have shared the personal data with the government or regulator. Keeping such segregation allows easy communication internally and externally.

Further, when publishing a privacy notice, consider using multiple communication channels. For instance, use emails, phone calls, SMS based notifications, etc.

Contrary to earlier recommendations of starting the work on certain tracks immediately and simultaneously, work on the privacy statement must wait for development of a clear approach on how you intend to manage consent and rights. Also, a review on data inventory can help.

Pro Tips

- A privacy statement (or notice) must be short (no more than 10 pages) and in customer-friendly, easily understood language. Legal jargon should not be used. Ideally a business stakeholder should write this and legal counsel should review it, not the other way around.

- A privacy statement is different from the terms and conditions for your products.
- The privacy statement must be easily accessible on your website.
- Privacy statements must be published for all data subjects (i.e., customers, employees and personnel of suppliers) to read.
- Publication of privacy statement is a mandatory legal requirement.
- The privacy statement is best published once your organization has a clear view on its overall GDPR approach and a clear strategy for aspects like consent, rights, data inventory, data expiration, legitimate purposes, etc. This is among

the later steps and may not be the first action to be worked upon.
- Be transparent and clarify sensitive topics like big data, profiling, selling of data, etc. It is better to say what it is one time, than have to answer for multiple requests when asked.
- To keep information accurate and up-to-date, update the privacy statement regularly. I recommend at least an annual review for most organizations.
- Be truthful and state the facts. Do not conceal information, because the purpose of a privacy statement (or notice) is transparency.
- The privacy statement (or notice) should be published in multiple languages (in line with what is common in your country).
- For both privacy statements and notices, you can be innovative and use

videos or animation to communicate with customers and create trust.

- Ask all your staff to read and understand the content of privacy statements and notices, so that they can answer queries verbally, if needed.

Note: If you would like to see examples of good and bad privacy statements, refer the UK Information Commissioner's office (the Privacy Commission equivalent of UK) website.

Chapter Eleven : Track 9: Create Awareness and Training

Objective: to help you build a comprehensive awareness and training plan that allows for embedding a culture of privacy and is not limited to one-off actions.

A core part of your GDPR implementation will include ensuring your employees understand the importance of data privacy and protection. Essentially, you need to ensure that data privacy and protection principles and processes are embedded in the day to-day activities of your business. This challenging aspect calls for implementing a culture (change) of privacy and ethics. While this is also a legal requirement, you need to build a comprehensive approach to:

- create awareness to ensure that all staff understand that privacy and protection of personal data are

important and the roles they play in GDPR compliance;
- provide basic information about data protection (and privacy) principles; and,
- clarify department-specific guidelines, especially regarding how to respond to a data subject query on privacy and protection

A simple approach entails planning activities with each of three above objectives in mind. Usually, each of these objectives can be separated or combined, based on the size and need of your organization. For the sake of simplicity, let us discuss the three objectives, one by one, as if you are managing these separately. This will allow you to understand better and choose what suits your organization best.

Awareness

Awareness is all about making sure that employees understand that privacy and protection of personal data is important and they each have a role to play. Ideally, this is best done if your messages demonstrate that privacy and protection have something to do with your business strategy. For example, if your company is bullish on digital or big data or analytics, then it is worthwhile to state that a crucial need to gain customer trust. For that, the company should be transparent in demonstrating that personal data is protected and privacy assured. To implement this objective, consider organizing events, sending messages, putting information on TV screens, etc. Asking each department's managers to organize dialogue sessions on how this can be relevant in their departments can also create awareness. This objective concerns all employees, and you should even include the staff of third party vendors that work for you.

Training

Training focuses on ensuring that all staff comprehend the minimum, basic information and know key concepts, like personal data, processor, controller etc.. At a minimum, this will include guidance on key concepts such as:

- What is personal data? What is sensitive data?
- Why is privacy and protection of this data important?
- How can this affect your business?
- What do you mean by privacy-by-design and default? How will each employee contribute towards this?

Of course, running them through the entire GDPR by means of a relevant example to your business can serve as one of many ideas. Should you choose to explain GDPR, I recommend using the building blocks described in Chapter 2 (*Chapter Two: GDPR Principles and Key Building Blocks*). Training can also be achieved with face-to-face sessions, e-learning, or any other mean that your company prefers. This objective pertains to all employees, and you should even include third party staff who work for you.

Guidelines

While sharing the importance of privacy and minimum knowledge about protection and privacy, most of your staff need clear and tangible direction on the changes GDPR compliance will make in their day-to-day lives. Typically, staff in human resources, procurement, sourcing, communication, and front offices are obvious candidates for dedicated training on:

- What are the dos and don'ts?
- What will change in their current way of working?
- What is the standard response to a customer who asks about his/her rights or receiving unsolicited emails etc.?

You don't have to make it complex, but embedding simple instructions like "You should read the privacy statement on our website" or "Send email to privacy@abccompany.com cannot do any damage and is strongly advised."

Although this sounds logical for banks, insurance companies, telecom providers, and some others, it may be challenging for other industries. For example, a retailer may not expect an employee sitting at the check-out counter to answer privacy questions. I like to challenge that view. Do you let the staff member sitting at the check-out counter copy credit card details? No, you do not. Most such operations already have a manual that already says that such action is against company policy and unethical. The point I emphasize is that GDPR creates the right opportunity to update staff guidelines. I am sure you don't want to pay a fine or suffer regulatory investigation because of this simple aspect.

In terms of timing, work on this track must wait for clarity to emerge from the other tracks. All the same, it can be helpful to start preparing and planning how you will execute awareness and training sessions. This is best conducted about three to four months before May 2018. Having said this, training for key staff who work on different parts of GDPR implementation should be conducted separately and needs to be scheduled at the start of the GDPR compliance effort. For such training, it is best to buy a generic GDPR training program from an external consultant firm or build a pack through the internal GDPR core team.

Pro Tips

- The law requires companies provide evidence on having trained staff on data protection and privacy. So, document your efforts.
- Do not underestimate the importance of planning and executing awareness sessions and training if your organization processes a significant amount of personal data.
- Save staff time by bundling training sessions and guidelines where possible. This way you manage the message in one iteration.

- Awareness and training on privacy and protection of personal data should be integrated as a regular activity embedded within your organization and adapted to the needs of major departments or functional roles.
- Using consultant(s) the first time around can be helpful, but you need to create knowledge in-house.

Chapter Twelve : Track 10: Manage Complaints and Breach

Objective: To provide you with an understanding on how to handle complaints and data breach notifications and the sources from which these can come.

Part of GDPR compliance includes an implementation plan that addresses the company's capability to manage complaints and breaches. While complaints are initiated by a data subject or supervisory authority, organizations are obligated to notify supervisory authorities or data subjects in case of a data breach. Let us understand each of these.

Complaints

GDPR provides data subjects with the right to file a complaint with a supervisory authority if the concerned data subject believes an organization has failed to comply with GDPR. To file a complaint, the data subject can approach the supervisory authority in member state of his residence, or place of his/her work, or place of alleged infringement. In addition, the data subject can pursue judicial remediation to obtain compensation for damages. Interestingly, a data subject can even lodge a complaint with the court against the supervisory authority when his/her complaint has not been addressed or the data subject has not been informed of progress on his/her case within three months of filing the initial complaint.

When a complaint is made in a country different than the country of the controller, then the supervisory authority of the country where controller has its main establishment becomes the "lead" supervisory authority. Other involved supervisory authorities become "non-lead." In such scenarios, the lead and non-lead must agree on who processes the complaint and refer the final decision to European Data Protection Board.

This means you need to prepare a mechanism to tackle complaints coming from the Data Protection Authority of any country in Europe. In addition, I recommend that your organization develops a method to allow data subjects to log data privacy complaints directly with you.

Data Breach

A data breach happens when security measures protecting personal data fail. That can result in the risk of unauthorized access, alteration, or destruction of data. This can be as simple as losing a laptop that contained the personal data of data subjects or illegal hacking of systems. When such breaches risk the rights and freedoms of individuals, the supervisory authority should be notified. And, in cases of high risk, even data subjects should be notified directly. Such notification must occur 72 hours of knowledge the breach.

While you implement a breach notification process, I strongly recommend splitting this into two stages:

1. Create an early notification process that allows you to comply within the 72-hour notification timeline. Such early notification can be as light as "We have evidence that a breach of such and such nature has happened. At present, we are investigating the impacted data subjects and consequences for them. We will notify you as we know more." We can argue that such early notification is not a good idea and may be a false alarm. But, being pragmatic, you must comply within 72 hours and prompt notification

will confer more credibility for being alert, even if the alarm is false. So, yes, it is possible to post early notifications. You can also state that the early notification was a false alarm and you discovered nothing.

- Provide a detailed notification when you have estimated the number of impacted data subjects and likely consequences affecting them. At this time, consider the aspect of notifying data subjects. The complete details should include the:
  - Number of personal records impacted
  - Number of data subjects impacted
  - Name and contact information of your Data Protection Officer
  - Description of likely impact of the data breach

- Proactive description of measures that were in place to prevent such breaches
- Lessons learned and the new measures that you will install to prevent reoccurrence.

As part of implementation, separate from the definition of the process, you should:

- Define templates for notification of a breach to the data protection authority and also to data subjects. Ideally, you should consider making two templates: one for early notification and one for complete details.
- Define key criteria on which you will base the decision to notify (or not) the data protection authority or data subjects.

- Decide on stakeholders who will validate these decisions. A DPO plays a significant role in this exercise.

In terms of timing, work on your approach towards complaints and breach can begin immediately. This is best done by a team that specializes in process management. Of course, collaboration with key stakeholders is vital. It is also likely to identified in the business gap analysis.

Pro Tips

- Most people are concerned about the 72-hour period, particularly when notification period starts. The GDPR clearly requires that you should send notification within 72 hours of detecting a breach. As soon as you know that a breach has happened, the clock starts to tick.

Be Ready for GDPR

- Adopt a principle of transparency and always consider providing an early notification of breach to your data protection authority as soon as you know about it. Doing so allows you to comply within the 72-hour notification period and should create trust.
- Be transparent with customers and encourage them to log privacy related complaints directly with you. While this creates trust and demonstrates accountability, it also allows you to sort data subject concerns directly and avoid complaints coming through a supervisory authority.
- Keep a register of personal data related complaints and breaches to record all such incidents.
- Keep evidence of the rationale used when you choose not to notify a supervisory authority of a data breach

Chapter Thirteen : Track 11: Sustainability

Objective: To guide you to longer term thinking that allows for compliance actions to remain sustainable and valid after the project winds down.

If I were to pick the most important track in the GDPR implementation, this is it. Making sure that actions taken in the prior tracks are sustained in the long term is critical to remaining compliant. So, let us begin by understanding what I mean by *sustainability*.

Sustainability is the perspective of looking forward (a few years) beyond the scope of your project or program and finding answers to the following three questions:

1. How will this organization remain compliant?

2. What are the actions required to remain compliant?
3. Who will take those actions? And, how will these actions be monitored?

GDPR is not about one-off implementation. It aims to embed a culture of privacy, so ensuring compliance on an ongoing basis is essential. Ensuring the sustainability of compliance impacts the policies, governance, people, processes, and systems in your organization. Let us dive deeply into each of these dimensions and explore what would change, why, and how you can make the change sustainable.

Governance

The first and foremost action to make GDPR implementation sustainable is to consider setting up a privacy office with a clear mandate. For small organizations, this responsibility can be fulfilled by a (possibly outsourced) Data Protection Officer; however, large organizations need dedicated manpower. Large organizations will require a team of specialists who can answer questions on privacy and protection and ensure that processes are followed, data breaches are registered and reported, etc.

Next, as you set up the privacy office, you cannot wash your hands of the compliance effort and say the privacy office staff will do everything. It is imperative to make clear that all staff, especially senior managers, have an important role to play. The other tracks covered earlier assure participation and communicate a clear mandate for action.

Having said that, as you set up the privacy office, define how privacy issues will be identified, approved, escalated, and resolved. While identification is ensured through staff, especially through an alert senior manager, approval, escalation, and resolution are achieved by creating a privacy board with competent senior managers from legal, risk, compliance, and security departments being involved, along with the DPO and the lead of the privacy office.

If your organization already has a strong data management department, then embed the privacy office into that department. Alternate options include establishing a security office or this being one of teams on chief operating officer's staff.

Policies

In Chapter 3 (*Chapter Three: Track 1: Put the Basics in Place*), I recommended that large organizations define a policy for personal data privacy and protection. Most global organizations already have policies and guidelines on security, risk management, data management, etc. It is extremely difficult to imagine that parts of these policies will not be impacted. Some of the existing polices may be less affected, while others would be more greatly impacted. But, if your organization wants to ensure that it remains complaint, then these policies cannot exist in isolation.

GDPR is here to stay. I strongly recommend, especially for large and global organizations, reviewing and refining existing policies where applicable. While it is difficult to start everything in parallel and change the entire organization at once, this effort would certainly need to be prioritized and planned in terms of actions prior and post May 25, 2018. Now, you may say that doing so would lead to the risk of not being fully compliant. And, I would challenge by asking, "Are you sure you will or are able to be fully compliant on May 25, 2018?" So, start planning for actions beyond May 25, 2018.

Processes

Although the different tracks described earlier emphasize that processes need to be created or modified, sustainable implementation may require some adaptations to the existing business and IT processes. Following is list of processes you may need to modify or develop:

- To keep information accurate and up-to-date, a process to regularly update privacy statement(s) is required. I would recommend at least an annual review for most organizations.
- The process to review design may require an added step to determine privacy-by-design guidelines have been factored into existing or new processes.
- To detect privacy incidents, your incident management process may need

fine-tuning to ensure data breaches are detected and reported.

- To ensure new subscribers /customers of services are made aware of privacy, new subscriber information may need to include privacy-related knowledge.

Systems in IT

Sustaining an effective GDPR implementation is likely to require execution of new systems or the installation of tools. Although the market may not offer many mature options, tools in following areas will certainly be required in the longer term:

- To maintain and govern personal data inventory
- To centralize, monitor and review privacy impact assessment gaps
- To manage consent

- To register and review complaints and data breach.

As I conclude this track, I acknowledge that some of you may feel that this is mostly applicable to large, global organizations, because small organizations will rely on a DPO to perform most of these tasks or expect other senior management to take on the additional responsibility.

In terms of timing, work on your approach towards sustainability can and should start when the gap analysis report is completed. The work is distributed across teams and generally spread across departments.

Pro Tips

- Don't buy tools for GDPR compliance yet. Let the market mature in coming years, and then buy what you need in a few years. Avoid making investments

that you may regret in the future. However, do explore the market and test the available options if you find them a fit for your needs.
- Data protection and privacy is an ongoing effort. The project or program will end, but efforts to remain compliant will continue.

Chapter Fourteen: Moving Forward with Your GDPR Compliance Plan

Objective: In this chapter, you will learn about how to leverage the knowledge and guidance acquired in previous chapters and receive suggestions for immediate action to take.

Now that you understand GDPR and have a perspective on the key tracks that should be part of a pragmatic GDPR implementation, it is time to revisit the different tracks and the objectives of each.

#	Track	Objective
1	Put the basics in place	To lay a strong foundation for your privacy and protection program.
2	Privacy-by-design	To define the privacy-by-design guidelines for your organization.
3	Data inventory	To take an inventory of personal data that exists in your organization.
4	Data expiration	To define an approach and plan for the expiration of data that is no longer relevant.
5	Consent	To define and implement an approach for consent in line with GDPR.

#	Track	Objective
6	Data subject rights	To define and implement an approach for rights in line with GDPR
7	Data transfers	To ensure the necessary safeguards are in place to protect individuals' rights and comply with GDPR when transferring data within and outside the organization.
8	Demonstrate transparency	To ensure transparency towards data subjects through privacy statements.
9	Create awareness and training	To ensure relevant staff understand data privacy and protection.

#	Track	Objective
10	Manage complaints and data breaches	To define and implement processes to handle complaints and data breaches.
11	Sustainability	To ensure that compliance is sustained beyond the initial compliance activities.

Table: Summary of tracks

With these tracks and the knowledge that you acquired in earlier chapters, I firmly believe that you are adequately equipped to either review your existing GDPR compliance plan or build a new one from scratch. Let us review these two situations.

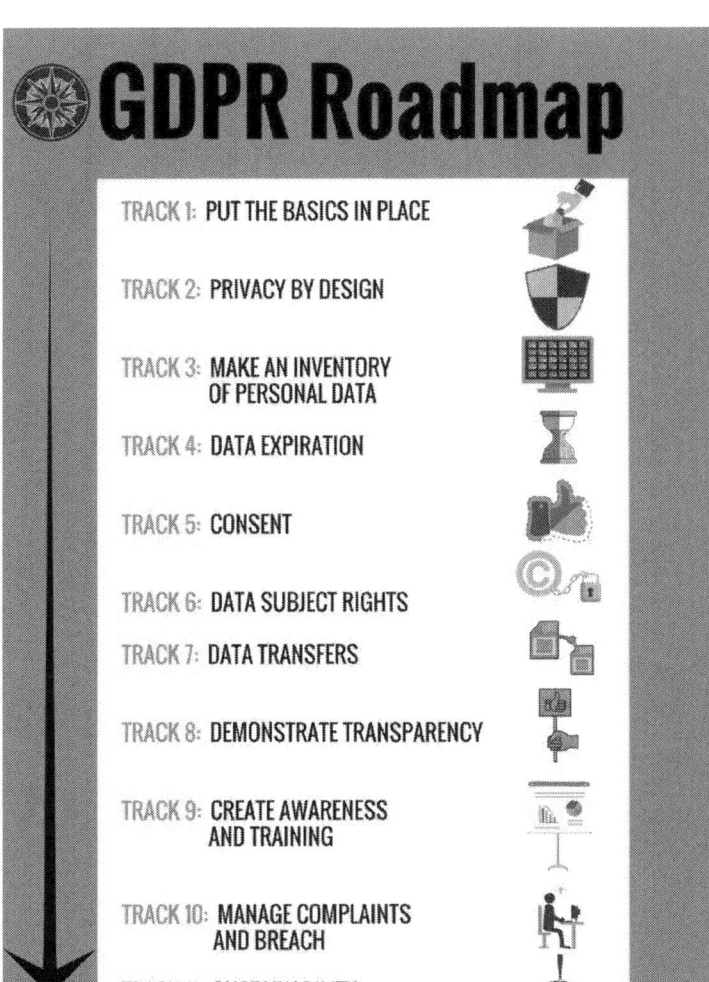

Image: Key tracks to consider in a GDPR roadmap

You don't have a plan yet

If you don't have a plan, it is best to start with Track 1 and review with your core team on which other tracks will be relevant in the context of your organization. It is possible you may want to cluster some of the tracks or even split them in line with your needs. This will allow you to make a plan and begin action. With less than one year left for compliance to GDPR, your focus should be on achieving following outcomes:

- The business gap analysis is completed and actions are prioritized. Gaps with highest risk are closed.
- An inventory of data is in place and expiration actions are initiated.
- Consent and rights processes are clarified and implemented.
- All staff is aware about data privacy, and key staff are trained on

implementation. Also, customer relations personnel should be equipped to answer customer queries on rights.

- A privacy statement is published.
- Contracts with third parties are amended for GDPR compliance needs.
- Data breach register is in place, and you are ready to detect and inform the Data Protection Authority about a breach, if required.
- A core group of stakeholders to act, in case of a privacy issue, like a data breach, is identified and prepared for any situation.
- The DPO is assigned, if necessary.
- All decisions made are documented.

Businesses that don't yet have a plan will find full compliance challenging; therefore, it is a good idea to prioritize on what can be done and what actions will continued after May 25,

2018. More importantly, regular follow-up and monitoring are required to ensure that you are in a position to answer the queries (if asked) posed by individuals and supervisory authorities.

You have a plan

If you do have a plan, then it is possible that you have different structure or approach to implementation. You do not have to change your structure. Just ensure that relevant aspects are covered, and validate that one or more key aspects have not been missed. For this, it is best to conduct a full-day workshop with your core team and verify that all aspects stated in different tracks of this book exist in your current plan. The possible outcomes from such a workshop can be broadly classified as follows:

1. Your plan includes all the stated aspects. In this case, be proud that

your plan is a good one. The next step is to ensure that planned actions are completed before May 25, 2018.
2. You plan did not include some of the aspects stated in this book. In this case, you must ensure that there is a valid reason for non-inclusion or include the relevant aspects in you plan. This means you must modify your plan and implement new actions.

While you are ahead of the game because you have a plan, it is still difficult to state whether you will be complaint or not by May 25, 2018. However, it is equally relevant for those who do not have a plan to act to ensure the necessary outcomes. For reference, checklists have been provided for you in the appendices. These can help you check off the key elements. Some points in the checklists may not be applicable to your organization, but I believe you are better off with these than without.

Pro Tips

- Your GDPR implementation will not end on May 25, 2018. So, identify what you will certainly need to do before May, 2018, and what can be done afterwards.
- As May 25, 2018, will be an important milestone in your GDPR compliance, focus on "must have" elements only. Typically, all the changes that involve customer interaction or that need interaction with the data protection authority should be assigned the highest priority.
- Plan for an external audit/certification on your organization's data protection situation around May, 2018, so that you

can reprioritize the actions to maintain compliance.

Chapter Fifteen: Critical Success Factors in Implementing GDPR Successfully

Objective: In this chapter, you will understand the do's, don'ts, and common mistakes that one can make while implementing GDPR.

Now that you have insight into the key aspects of GDPR and its implementation tracks, let me share the critical success factors that will help you ensure you do the right things and avoid common mistakes.

1. Look at GDPR as a framework that allows you and your organization to build and develop its own approach for protecting personal data. This is the most critical element, because I have seen people expecting clear and

specific instructions. In my opinion, the framework does not have to be precise, but clear enough to define your privacy strategy so that you can not only demonstrate compliance to law, but also create a competitive advantage for your organization. In short, do not see this as ceiling under which you should fit, but a floor on which you can build and engage your customers to do business and to increase their trust.

2. Understand the role of your organization as controller or processor of personal data for various data, and then define what aspects of GDPR would apply to your organization on which types of data. Almost all organizations will serve as controller of their employees' data, but not all organizations can be the controller of

their customers' data. Hence, it is best to align with key stakeholders, preferably at the executive committee level, and agree on these roles.

3. Compliance with the law and avoidance of fines are certainly important, but only focusing on those sets yourself up for challenges in longer term. Instead, I strongly recommend taking a longer term perspective and looking at sustainable actions that not only create compliance by May 25, 2018, but also ensure continuing compliance afterward.

4. GDPR implementation is not a step-by-step process, but consists of steps that run mostly parallel with each other and are iterative in nature. Therefore, you are better off working

in agile mode and managing this as a large program to protect personal data.

5. Data protection is not about technological change. It focuses on governance and business, with technology enabling some of the choices your business will make. I have seen organizations start with the thought that this will be a technical implementation and eventually realize that this is more of a business change and less of an IT change.

6. Your legal counsel is an advisor. Use him/her as your guide once you have an approach or idea, but not as an instructor specify your action. This is very important, because I have seen managers ask legal counsel what they should do and then not be happy with the answers. The reason is that if you ask a wrong question to the wrong

person, then you are bound to get the wrong answer. It is the responsibility of business to decide how to operate the business and the responsibility of legal counsel to advise if such operation is within the law or not.

7. Like any other strategic initiative, it is critical to engage the right stakeholders for this effort. For a large organization, such stakeholders may include representatives from business operation, marketing, data, legal, risk, compliance, architecture, IT, security, and project/program management. For small organizations, consider these as input perspectives you would need and think about who would provide these insights.

8. GDPR knowledge in market is scarce. So, you need to look for smart people who can understand core concepts,

synthesize different aspects of the law, and communicate to a variety of people (e.g., lawyers, architects and business executives) in their languages, while remaining simple and relevant. Look for people who love challenge, learn fast, and dare to be creative. Basically, you need people with "can do" attitude and the willingness to learn. I am not saying don't hire externally, but I am recommending that you build knowledge internally and make decisions internally while taking advantage of consultant expertise to deliver specific outcomes where knowledge is a commodity. For example, a consultant can perform a business gap analysis or privacy impact assessment knowledge.

9. GDPR in itself is important, but exclusive focus on GDPR is not ideal. While your privacy project or program should implement data protection and privacy with GDPR as its core, your program should also consider and incorporate other laws in conjunction with GDPR. For example, a look into e-privacy regulation currently being drafted can help avoid the need to develop a new program in coming years.

10. GDPR can seem like it impacts all aspects of your organization. Try to focus on keeping things simple where possible. Do not write new policies every time. Instead, look for existing policies that can be amended. Some consultants may advise you to write a new policy or procedure every time,

but use your common sense and avoid work for colleagues when you can.

In summary, GDPR implementation is not about one-off compliance action in terms of technology, but about strategic governance and business choices that have a longer-term impact on your business and that determine how you engage your customers through a transparency approach that wins more business by differentiation from the competition. Be aware that GDPR will impact all layers of your organization; i.e., it will impact the processes, policies, governance, and even your organizational structure.

And, the golden rules of "Don't fix it unless it's broken," "Keep it simple and stupid," etc. will help you immensely. For now, start implementing because you may already be very late.

Pro Tips

- Structure your GDPR implementation. This gets clearer as you read through the earlier chapters that elaborated on tracks that you should consider.
- GDPR implementation is not about one-off actions, but concerns a longer-term perspective.
- GDPR is not an IT implementation project; It will touch all aspects across your organization.
- Do not seek GDPR consultants, create GDPR knowledge based on a commonsense approach.
- The time to May 25, 2018, grows short. Schedule your planning activities for each month and review progress on a weekly or biweekly basis. You must be

in position to answer customer requests regarding their rights and inform regulators of a data breach.

One last thing…

Privacy is a new topic and will evolve over time. In my view, the next five years or so will witness a lot of new developments, tools, and skills. If you are working on this topic, enjoy development of these new skills, because privacy is most likely here to stay.

With this, I hope you found this book useful. I wish you success with your GDPR compliance. Please take the time to share your feedback and suggestions on Amazon. That would be highly appreciated.

You can also contact me on social media and use #beReadyforGDPR to tweet.

Appendices

1. Checklist for Senior Managers/Executives

To ensure privacy and protection on an ongoing basis:

#	Requirement	Yes/No
1	A business gap analysis has been performed for my division/department.	
2	All gaps identified from business gap analysis have been closed.	
3	I have installed a Data Privacy Impact Assessment procedure and ask for Data Privacy Impact Assessments when a new initiative with risk to individual rights is being launched.	

#	Requirement	Yes/No
4	For initiatives that include the processing of personal data, I inquire as to whether they comply with privacy-by-design principles.	
5	For initiatives that include processing of personal data, I ask whether such processing has a legitimate purpose, if there is another reason for processing, or if it requires consent.	
6	My staff are aware of the relevance and significance of personal data privacy and protection principles.	
7	When in doubt, I contact my organization's Data Protection Officer.	

2. Checklist for Assurance of a Comprehensive GDPR Implementation Plan

To review the GDPR situation that you have and find challenges with current plan.

#	Requirement	Yes/No
1	A Data Protection Officer has been assigned and mandated.	
2	A cross-functional team to work on GDPR implementation is in place.	
3	Governance: A steering committee to drive GDPR implementation is in place and includes stakeholders from legal, risk, business, and IT teams	

#	Requirement	Yes/No
4	A GDPR program plan exists and the relevant budget is approved.	
5	Privacy-by-design guidelines are being prepared (or are available).	
6	A privacy impact assessment template and process are being installed.	
7	A business gap analysis has been (or will be) performed for all departments.	
8	A technical gap analysis has been (or will be) performed for all applications/systems that process personal data.	

#	Requirements	Yes/No
9	All staff have been (or will be) trained and made aware of the principles concerning privacy and protection of personal data.	
10	A personal data inventory has been (or will be) prepared and will include the purposes for which we process it and the relevant retention period of such data.	
11	An approach to respect individual rights requests has been (or will be) implemented.	

#	Requirements	Yes/No
12	My organization has (or will have) an approach for consent management, and the same has been (or will be) implemented.	
13	Processing of children's data has been (or is being) reviewed in line with GDPR.	
14	An approach for notification of a data breach to the data protection authority or the individuals concerned has been (or is being) prepared.	

#	Requirements.	Yes/No
15	Third parties that process personal data for us know their responsibilities and their contracts have been amended accordingly	
16	Data transfers within entities of our corporate company are formalized.	
17	Personal and sensitive data classification is known and documented.	
18	Unless legally required, personal data is no longer retained once its legitimate purpose is completed.	

#	Requirements	Yes/No
19	IT systems have implemented data protection principles as listed in our privacy-by-design guidelines.	
20	Privacy governance to monitor compliance and resolve privacy issues is in place.	
21	A GDPR-compliant privacy statement for customers is published on our website.	
22	GDPR-compliant privacy statement for employees and supplier personnel is published on our intranet.	

#	Requirement	Yes/No
23	Individuals can log complaints to raise their personal data concerns.	
24	A process is in place to review the existing GDPR situation and find compliance challenges within our current plan	

3. Data Inventory Checklist

To review the GDPR data inventory template.

#	Requirement	Yes/No
1	Personal data is categorized.	
2	All personal data maps have a legitimate purpose.	
3	The legal and actual storage periods of all personal data are listed.	
4	External processing, when applicable, is indicated in data inventory.	
5	Ownership of each data element exists.	

4. Privacy Statement Checklist
To review the GDPR data inventory template.

#	Requirement	Yes/No
1	Customers are informed about what data you process.	
2	Customers are informed about why you process certain personal data.	
3	Customers are assured about personal data being safe and protected.	
4	External processing reasons and methods are shared.	
5	Ownership of each data element exists.	
6	Customers are informed of their privacy rights.	

#	Requirement	Yes/No
7	Data Protection Officer contact is provided to request more information.	

About the Author

Punit Bhatia is a senior professional with more than 18 years of experience in executing change and leading transformation initiatives. Across three continents, Punit has led projects and programs of varying complexity in business and technology throughout multiple industries. He has experience on both sides of the table; i.e., he has served as a consultant who worked for IT consulting companies, and also as a key influencer and driver who has defined and delivered change for large enterprises. He has proven expertise in areas of data privacy, sourcing and vendor management, and digital transformation.

For last two years, he has been driving the compliance with **General Data Protection Regulation** (GDPR) in a large bank. Part of this effort entails attendance in multiple events and dialogue with many experts. He has acquired knowledge and expertise in the field of data privacy and protection. Consequently, he is now active as a GDPR expert as a speaker or panelist at different events. At present, he is also busy developing a privacy vision across multiple countries for his employer.

Acknowledgements

Andre Luc Bisson, for reviewing the draft book and providing valuable insights.

Bert van de Haar, for reviewing the draft book.

Erik Luysterborg, for reviewing the draft book and providing remark on book relevance.

Elizabeth Venneks Kelly, for sharing her experiences in writing a book.

Marc Vanvilthoven, for sowing the inspiration to be an expert.

Namita Bhatia (my wife), for being patient with my ideas.

Yash Bhatia (my son), for bringing new ideas and energy when book was being written.

And special thanks go to all my family, parents, colleagues, and friends who stand by me, work with me, and challenge me to learn every day. Most importantly, all those on LinkedIn who advised on choice of cover and shared their views.

Printed in Poland
by Amazon Fulfillment
Poland Sp. z o.o., Wrocław